BOTTLE THE BOTTLES THE BOTTLES THE BOTTLES

CLEVELAND STATE UNIVERSITY POETRY CENTER
NEW POETRY

Caryl Pagel, Series Editor

Michael Dumanis, Founding Series Editor

Samuel Amadon, *The Hartford Book*
John Bradley, *You Don't Know What You Don't Know*
Lily Brown, *Rust or Go Missing*
Elyse Fenton, *Clamor*
Emily Kendal Frey, *The Grief Performance*
Lizzie Harris, *Stop Wanting*
Rebecca Hazelton, *Vow*
Chloe Honum, *The Tulip-Flame*
Rebecca Gayle Howell, *Render / An Apocalypse*
Lesle Lewis, *A Boot's a Boot*
Dora Malech, *Say So*
Siwar Masannat, *50 Water Dreams*
Shane McCrae, *Mule*
Helena Mesa, *Horse Dance Underwater*
Philip Metres, *To See the Earth*
Broc Rossell, *Festival*
Zach Savich, *The Firestorm*
Sandra Simonds, *Mother Was a Tragic Girl*
S. E. Smith, *I Live in a Hut*
Mathias Svalina, *Destruction Myth*
Allison Titus, *Sum of Every Lost Ship*
Lee Upton, *Bottle the Bottles the Bottles the Bottles*
Liz Waldner, *Trust*
Allison Benis White, *Self-Portrait with Crayon*
William D. Waltz, *Adventures in the Lost Interiors of America*
Jon Woodward, *Uncanny Valley*
Wendy Xu, *You Are Not Dead*

For a complete listing of titles please visit
www.csupoetrycenter.com

BOTTLE THE BOTTLES THE BOTTLES THE BOTTLES

Lee Upton

Cleveland State University Poetry Center
Cleveland, Ohio

Copyright © 2015 by Lee Upton

ISBN 978-0-9860257-7-8

First edition

19   18   17   16   15   5   4   3   2   1

This book is published by the Cleveland State University Poetry Center,
2121 Euclid Avenue, Cleveland, Ohio 44115-2214
www.csupoetrycenter.com and is distributed by
SPD / Small Press Distribution, Inc. www.spdbooks.org.

Cover image: *Bottles* by Amy Freels, copyright © 2014, used with permission.
Bottle the Bottles the Bottles the Bottles was designed and typeset by Amy Freels in Joanna.

LIBRARY OF CONGRESS CATALOGING-IN-PUBLICATION DATA
Upton, Lee, 1953–
  [Poems. Selections]
  Bottle the bottles the bottles the bottles / Lee Upton. — First edition.
      pages ; cm. — (New poetry)
  ISBN 978-0-9860257-7-8 (acid-free paper)
  I. Title.

  PS3571.P46A6 2015
  811'.54— dc23

                    2015002240

Acknowledgments

The author thanks the editors of the following journals in which some of these poems, sometimes under different titles and in other versions, first appeared:

32 Poems, AGNI, Boston Review, Colorado Review, Connotations, Crazyhorse, Ecotone, Fairy Tale Review, FIELD: Contemporary Poetry and Poetics, Hamilton Stone Review, Harpur Palate, Life and Legends, Massachusetts Review, The New Republic, Plume, Reunion: The Dallas Review, River Styx, Roanoke Review, Sawbuck, Third Coast, TLR: An International Journal of Contemporary Poetry, and Verse.

"Drunk at a Party" first appeared in AGNI and was reprinted in Best American Poetry 2011.

Contents

—for two sisters: *Alesia Betz,* and in memory of *Carla Carter*

Pandora

Why expect me to open this?
What specific qualifications are required to open this?
What if I won't find what you expect when I open this?
What if it's pillars,
golden birds, the mountains,
and slow clover and snow cover,
ceilings clouded and only
a few broken shells, dust from a granary,
one broken spine when I open this?
Why expect me to be the one to open this?
Tell me again what specific qualifications are required
to open this.
Maybe something swarms
under the lid like ants.
Migrating ants. I open this.

Bottle the Bottles the Bottles the Bottles

I never thought I'd lie down.
Now I'm a ship in a bottle
getting nowhere fast.

My first mate: a fly
with a bucket of gear.
Bottles in and bottles out.

A bottle fly dies
with his pack crumpled on his chest.
Dust loves a bottle anywhere.

By firelight a bottle
looks full of fish.
Bottle the bottles the bottles.

If my ship sails
out of the bottle
and onto the shore

will the day glitter,
a breakable souvenir?
I doubt the one I love

can be pleased anyhow.
That man would criticize Vermeer
for the way the milk pours.

Drunk at a Party

He couldn't imagine it now,
kicking back,
wandering around with a glass,
weirdly morose or—what's the word?—
jolly. His voice sounding vaguely Swiss
or Peruvian or Dutch. Could he
pick up the rhythm
of the lush he once was,
get lugubrious with that woman
from the controller's office?
Break down, regret everything or—
the opposite—
boast?

What latch keeps a brain
from spinning like a prawn
dropped on a stranger's parquet?
Ages ago in a land far away
lucky people got three martinis for lunch.
Whole lifetimes hung on a ledge
disgorging the slippery
feelers of sloe gin. Who would he be
if he passed out again?
Or if love plucked his eyes
and made any throat glisten?
This descendant of men who broke
their necks
in buckets of hard cider?
Why am I speaking
at this moment
as if I were a man?

What am I guilty of?
What keeps a lobster
out of a tank?

Gorged

Birds, eels,

cheese in slabs high as a mortuary,

mussels that are knuckles nearly, the grouper

with its brain scooped out next to its eyes.

You're the cart and you're piled,

but when it comes to some meals

I'm a hermit who dines on

ice cubes—

my empire's gorged.

Of course I'm not talking about dinner.

I can choose a reason to live

from so many possibilities

but partway through a course

who doesn't grow unsatisfied?

Weren't even our first mistakes

copies of their original forms?

Every time I swallow

my philosophy hurts.

The Liar, Emily Dickinson

Who will answer her question?
The liar, Emily Dickinson.
The frogs call nobody's name—
although they live in a loud republic.

I unpeeled myself
from my own name—and now what?
There's a pair of me.
Don't tell? I'll tell everybody.

"During the Victorian Era Women Often Fell into Holes"

—draft of topic sentence, research report

All in a slump or adrift, without a ladder or a rope or a branch. Dangled
over the deepest pit, sister. Update the heretic's

fork with a whalebone corset. Your brother's in the mine shaft. You're
hurtling past

crockery. Not so fast. Syphilis and her sisters. Bobbing for clams. Backhoe
a grave, waiting for the pileup.

Down a hole then through the glass. Even the moon isn't spared. Pocked
and scratched. Finger all the

stops in a word. Go flat. Girdle the mast. A disaster inside a disaster's
another disaster.

Watch that, sister. Hide with your horse in a ditch.
Twist out of plaster

every other sister. Choke-hold every hole as she goes. The paper wears thin the eraser.

Pump up the drum. If she plummets tell her to plummet faster. Make a hole to last her.

Ode on "Ode on a Grecian Urn"

Party-goers,
foster children of Xanax,
around and around and around they go,

breathing for us, breathing
and thirsty
on their way out of town.

It's never not spring.
It's a festival where
nothing amounts to kissing.

No one drinks from anyone's lips.
No one drinks.
Blood flecks a pillowcase,

and the pillow is turned over.
Then the head stays. Truth loves Beauty,
and Beauty hides his face.

The Mermaids Sang to Me

And I was inside their song.
Until at last I began to think:
they're a bunch of bores.

I must send them packing,
them and their aureoles.
Their eyes, shark dead,

their hides like stamp pads and arrowheads.
Odysseus should have tied them to the mast first
for the crime of singing so much

about their own lives.
Just then, the moon came out in clouds
shaped like Annabel Lee,

and the ghost of Edgar Allan Poe
bobbed in the mirror above my buffet.
If you want the truth, the ghost said,

don't look in the mirror.
The mermaids are shrinking, turning transparent,
setting up their grottos in daiquiris.

You must prefer the window to the mirror.
The window, dappled with liver spots.
(To which the mirror replied: No one is fair to me.)

Dewiest

...dew, dew dresses, stones and chains of dew, heads
Of the floweriest flowers dewed with the dewiest dew.
—Wallace Stevens

One misty moisty morning...
—Nursery rhyme

Our dew was the dewiest.
We were posted against flooding

and drenched in the drenchiest frocks.
We were strolling, standing, strapping dew,

dew beyond the grass slip, dew to dip
under the lips of seraphim,

like a near-cliché that never gets
rooted in common parlance.

Our dew dresses, our slips of dew,
our dew that in its depths

lodges the glacier's aspirations,
the wettest opal to rival reason,

the dewiest dresses, the dew of dresses,
the dew that drew the misty morning

when the men were forsaking leather.
The dues of yesteryear.

Dewy and dewier and dewiest.
Yet another mermaid who kept bad company

on one of our high level mornings
right when we were beading up.

The Age of Beauty

I hope we can rescue Beauty from the mountain pass
        before parts of him are to be sewn shut,
                for he is beautiful on the mountain pass.

They say even the soap he washes with dirties his hands.
        He's so beautiful there are those who want him
            to walk inside a shroud

and never leave the mountain pass.
        And now that Beauty is tied up on the mountain pass
            we ought to put our backpacks on and
            rescue him

so that he can walk down the mountain by himself
        on his tiny twice bound feet.
           Oh, Beauty, let us rescue you

from your beautiful self
        in the name of your body. (Poor body,
           everybody has ideas about you.)

Marsyas

To have been proud

to have dared

that sensitivity and need and now

to be rigged upside down

without meaning against meaning

the body freckled like

the inside of a fox glove

skin not to be slipped off

so easily not a glove of skin

the web of him

first his eyelids peeled

so he will see everything

done to him

blood filming his eyes

figs of blood

flies crawled

his spirit cannot walk across the field

and rest under the tree

to turn away from this work

his brain a Ferris wheel plunging until

he is dangling like

something in a butcher's window

his albatross body

they have baked a swan for later with wine

after the work of him

turning him into papyrus stamped

rolled the thistle down of his hair

fire saddles streaming

riveted and pleated

the grass pebbled

and then soaked flat

heart pumping through this

and the rags of him fluttering

what did they want with skin

a banner a flag

what does a god need with skin

what did an illusion do with you.

Grim Progress

[B]ut when they are by themselves, as the Robin, they can catch and gobble up
Spiders, they can change their diet, drink Iniquity, and swallow down Sin like water.
—The Pilgrim's Progress

We drink skim
and we drink fat.
We spin flies
from spiders.
We char snakeskin,
craters, bombers.
We swallow pills
and run for Congress.
We hire kin
and lure
for our bobbers.
We gobble ground
and diet on
lobsters.
We run guns.
We sink swallows.
We make sex
look like
gallows.
We dig hollows
in your
mountains.
We boil
filthy
words
with
breath.

We take up
all your
bandwidth.

No Thanks to You and Your Whiskey

Look. The Picts and the Huns blew in at last—
thanks to you and your whiskey.
Now your cow is in the corn.
You can blow your horn
but she'll shred the flags

of a thousand countries.
She thinks she's Marcus Aurelius
mowing barbarians down.
She's bloating and she won't budge.
That's the way I feel about libraries.

Thanks. The rhinoceros thinks she's a hippo
equipped for war.
No thanks. No thanks
to you and your whiskey.
Half the time I love actors.

Half the time I pretend to.
I auditioned but landed
in the crew. No thanks.
They say the more you drink
the thirstier your thinking.

I can't read the devil's handwriting
on this contract, can you?
His penmanship, all forks.
No thanks. No thanks to you
and your whiskey.

Tender is the Night

Succulents are rightly named,
reservoirs of the garden,
as if to say:
I keep my own
darkening well in reserve.
I love rain so much I barrel it.
Who wouldn't want,
like one of their kind,
to save what should be loved?
For instance, I'm placing
here that line
by Keats that Fitzgerald
himself saved: *Tender is the night.*
What's inside the deep night
inside of us?
Somewhere,
against all terrible predictions,
someone is saved.
I don't know how it happens.
How the night is tended.
How the night is tender.

Even If

The beautiful thing you did

that no one knows about

or forgot

or no one cares for—

it's there always:

light, grainy light—

it's there in that high room as a

light that guides from a great distance

ships at sea,

even if those ships aren't in our world—

even if those ships are

ghost ships,

they're guided

by the light of that beautiful thing,

even if cruelty gets its hands on it.

It's done.

You were born. No taking that back.

A Terrarium

Camouflaged, the ones near the path

in the overgrown meadow,

although you'll notice

the armory of thistles

and the tiger lilies

billowing in the ditches.

My sister would crawl down to listen,

she said, to the grass growing or the moss, wild

and greener

than any other,

the moss I wanted

for a terrarium.

*

We lived among wild flowers

with weeds carpeting the meadow,

persistent like our ancestors—the long-lived

and the long-suffering, and my sister

collected their histories:

the baby said to have

suffocated in bed,

a grandmother wandering

on the road in winter

wearing only her nightgown

sleeved in ice,

our own mother waiting

on the hospital steps

during our brother's operation.

When she walked up to her father's room—

he was being treated

in the same hospital for his asthma—

she found him dead.

I could have been with him, she said,

the whole time I waited on the steps.

Nearly every week of her life

my mother drew pictures of her sister

who died at three months and a day

four years before our mother's own birth.

A face she'd never seen but drew.

The baby's name was Laura.

*

The deaths spread forward and back.

My mother's sister's first child: polio.

Her great uncle who kept the eye of her doll

when his sister Anna died—

twelve years and two days old: typhoid.

Now I have the table my mother learned to write on:

a rope table it's called.

Needed at home, my mother was out of school

by the time she was thirteen.

When my mother's brother was being born

her mother was told

the doctor would have to take him

"leg by leg, arm by arm" to save her life.

She wouldn't let the doctor

and lived. Pernicious anemia,

cerebral hemorrhage.

A baby who weighed

sixteen pounds, her mother a hundred.

The barn burned three times.

Chronic asthma.

Vascular dementia.

The blood clot traveled.

The broken neck.

The one who left camp

when men thawed dynamite in a stove.

The other men perished.

The one who produced silent movies,

frozen out when talkies came in.

My father who fell down a hay shaft

and spent seven weeks in bed with a flat iron.

My sister kept the records:

she herself survived cancer and surgery and then

multiple pneumonias.

Even to strangers she seemed to be

a friendly and brave woman.

Admitted to the hospital.

Discharged. Readmitted for pneumonia.

Sedated for many days. Then she began recovering.

Suffered a stroke, perhaps from medication.

Again, began her recovery.

Then she was discharged

from the hospital and died.

*

The milkweed sprayed light,

and the buckhorn plantain set up camp,

secured by a taproot like a tent peg.

These tarnished

companions in arms. How many wands

of Queen's Anne's lace did we bring home?
The house we grew up in
on its way to becoming a ruin.

*

My mind needs to travel
farther than it has traveled,
but I keep remembering
standing in snow with our sleds,
needles of snow in both our faces.
We are laughing so hard snow is landing in our mouths.
She endured our mother's death
just months before her own.

*

Twice in one day on different islands
under vines, the light flares
through the fine early leaves.
Looking up: a bower
unfolding like
green green green
tender paper, green as the album

in which my sister

created the family history,

the leaves uncurling, sun scrolls.

*

Before our mother's death I had a fantasy:

that she would be strong again.

I played around with Keats

and "La Belle Dame Sans Merci."

Except I would call my piece

"La Belle Dame Sans Her Tea."

I was writing that my mother was

discharged,

discharged as if catapulted

out of the ward

and back into a kimono

of cranes and snow drops.

So where was her tea?

Every season is two seasons:

spring and snowdrops.

I couldn't finish.

I tried other possibilities:

First put the kettle on and let it boil

like hail sizzling

and at last pour the heated water

into a cup

and bring the cup

on a saucer

and let her handle it: a triumph.

She lifted her own cup!

Lifted with her small human hand

and her mind brightening

after the nightmare of the glacier,

after the birds sing and the sedge unwithers.

We cool the tea first

so as not to scald her.

It was my sister, not my mother, lifting a cup

which made us believe she was recovering.

*

She did not pity herself.

Go on. Work. Don't indulge.

Your old habits come first.

You're meant to span the bridge.

You should learn a few things:

the doctor said

one lung must be smaller than the other

to accommodate her heart.

*

She could hardly breathe

when she phoned me.

She called to say a family she worked with

was featured in a television show.

The family was filmed getting a new house.

Her voice—a whisper through feathers.

*

The painting in my older daughter's room:

scarred at the lake in the center,

the lake by the mountains

near the meadow of wild flowers.

You can see right there at the center where

when I was a girl

I threw an ashtray at my sister and missed her.

She visited when my mother lived with us

and we hardly knew she was in the house.

She didn't want to be entertained.

She sat beside my mother,

who was steadily going blind,

tying bits of satin.

As girls we fought. She bossed me.

I chased her with sleigh bells, with scissors.

She laughed at me.

I was enraged by her.

I was four years younger.

I gave up dolls to be like her.

I thought that I could be like her.

Our mother's death in May,

our niece's in June,

my sister's in January.

While she was in the hospital

she kept calling for our mother

and then said she really meant

to call for her husband

but our mother's name

came out of her mouth.

She was fearless. Here she is

in majorette camp.

Here she is with a motorcycle.

Here she is saying to me, Breathe,

just breathe.

Here she is with her doll Betty.

Here we are in the snowstorm.

*

After a woman wrote of her husband's death

someone said, Why write that?

Does she think

she's the only one

who's ever

gone through that?

But couldn't that be said

of anything?

I wanted to defend the woman who

wrote about her husband

but, then, I wasn't myself.

*

My Uncle Fergus—the one the doctor wanted

to take leg by leg and arm by arm—grew Japanese lantern flowers

beside his porch.

Each looked like an inflated orange sack,

or a tiny canteen,

or a shrunken tent

where a general drafts war plans.

Or the swelling interior

of a sunlit heart, beating,

saving as if for an emergency

one precious bubble of air.

*

I came down the stairs

and for minutes I thought they were with me,

my mother and sister.

I had been hopeful

when my sister came to herself

after sedation.

I wrote:

It's New Year's Day and one of us is almost out of the woods,

touching the tree trunks as she goes.

She is wandering barefoot in snow.

It's on our fingertips too, the rough bark she steadies against.

She feels her way across the dark,

even as, here, the snow falls.

I didn't write more at the time.

Snow against our faces,

snow needles pierced our eyelids.

*

I said I'd see her in the summer

for a visit

and believed myself.

A few years ago

she sent me paper she had made.

Some little flecks like

roots pressed inside each sheet.

I remember how burdocks caught in our hair.

We walked among weeds

that thrived on neglect.

Later I learned the names of thistles:

star thistle,

milk thistle,

cotton thistle.

Why an early death?

The sumac like antlers,

the velvet never

rubbed off. At twilight by the canal locks

there were a few instants

when the sky seemed flat

before the deeper darkness soaked in,

the color coming from behind it.

*

My sister was kind.

She never wasted things.

I wasted many things.

I made many terrariums.

She helped me with my life.

I helped her with her spelling.

I read and read and read and read

and in reading I hoped and hope for . . .

Although they never met,

and had spoken only once by phone,

Elizabeth Bishop gave

a bottled cross to Flannery O'Connor.

Washed in from Brazil

and encased in glass,

the bottled cross is made up of

an altar, a ladder,

and a cross carved from wood.

Atop the cross perches a paper rooster

as delicate as a thistle.

On the ladder to the cross

the implements of torture are hung

and are useless: the body's

off the cross.

The body that bottles agony.

Far Country

When you were in that country
I didn't feel you were far away.
You were close, even though
you were in that far country,
and then when I visited you in that country
I saw how far away you'd been,
how in that country by the North Sea
the winds buffeted you, cold winds,
and you walked on the cliff side,
as if clover could raise the sea.
You swayed within that country far away.
I can say that now,
after seeing the white-washed store fronts,
the trees loosening every wind in that country.
Even now I think of you walking on a ledge
in that far country,
the waves coming in as pages of books, not dreams
but actual pages,
and the pages are the blue of long life,
and the pages open endlessly
turned by an invisible hand.
You walk that ledge in that far country
above a sea unfolding depths,
raising and lowering waves
shining at night as books in silver rows
in that far country
where you are and must be
a woman and a Prospero.

The Immortal Orchard

No one will ever be hungry here.

The fruit that lodged Persephone in hell,
and figs, and olives, and apples

cling like bats at a cave wall.
A branch springs back and shudders

with blossoms unfolding into pears.
The orchard bears fruit all year,

and once he's under those branches,
Odysseus doesn't consider how

he will be battered into an old man.
He doesn't wonder about his friends

twisting in the wind, not when he's beneath
planets bunched in glittering air,

not when he stares at an archipelago of lures,
an ageless fountain, an undimmed mirror.

Just the same, even he turns his back.
Even he walks away

from unending, griefless, alien replenishment.
And like a hero of our own

he comes to us at home,
toward our faces looming in rows,

and won't let us die by ourselves.

The Committee

I formed a committee.
As a consequence I was
forlorn as a committee.

The truth is
I can't get along in a committee.
I'm already a committee.

I'm a committee in a committee.
Don't expect me to run the committee.
Watch the committee try to run by me.

If you think oyster bars are cheap
you've never been in one
in a committee.

The last memorandum
by the committee was so numbing
it took a head wound

for the committee.
Oh, cabbages of regret,
Oh, desperate histories

of all committees
since the world began,
today the rain is as sparkling

as Keats rolling over in bed.
He was extraordinarily good looking,
according to the committee.

Did he appoint the committee?
The good thing is:
the committee has advanced a motion

to disband itself as a committee.
Thank you, members of the committee.
Thank you for your labors,

many and wonderful and sundry.
Thank you on behalf of the committee.

Antlers in the Conference Room

It's not loud at first around a crowd of us,
more like walnuts clacking in a wooden bowl.
But then the antlers lock in the archway
and lay waste to the chandelier,
and we're casting shadows until
the ceiling is an incised atelier,
and we're hot flank to hot flank,
some of us convinced our heads
deserve to be mounted
above a blueprint.
Whereas, frankly,
I, for one, increasingly would like to crash
through a forest, any forest,
or forklift snow with my impressive gear.
Or just stand here lifting,
a weight lifter when it comes to my head:
I can't help my head,
if the same arguments grow out of it.

Melting & Shrieking

She's un-meated and de-greened
and de-cheated,
she's anti-freeze,
a puddle gone under,
a shrinking disease.
She's the splatter guard,
a bat in a slump.
She's punked.
That's that.
She's flatter than flat.
We poured cold water on her.
We made a bong out of her.
She's a spine of brine, an ink track.
Sizzling stir fry. Hello, goodbye.
Sister-less, sockless,
pocket-less, clock-less.
Rolled and filleted,
snow in a fireplace,
sand in a wave.
Her tongue steams fast:
complaint and wonder
taken under.
Now we're marooned here.
Her dragoons here.
We're still in trenches
no one mentions.

"Today is the Anniversary of Today"

And tomorrow is the anniversary of tomorrow,
and yesterday is the anniversary of
the steam engine marrying
rural electrification

and Genghis Khan learning to toddle on a horse.
History is ideas and consequences.
Someone humiliates himself.
Someone makes a miracle shove maggots into her mouth.

Love's Ode

There once was a man who loved me
with a cat's love,
which is to say I could not depend on it,
although I could depend on his punctuality.

A cat's appetite is a clock.
There once was a clock
who loved me like a man.
Not like any man

but like one particular man.
A clock has time on its hands,
and you can tell time's up by its face.
There once was a face

that loved me like a suitcase,
a suitcase on the conveyor belt
forgotten for two weeks at the airport.
There once was a man

who loved me like an airport.
I had to take off my clothes
just to get past security.
There once was security

in loving no one at all.
No one at all was enough for me.
Then I bought a cat.
A man appeared who loved me

as if he loved me.
Love was a cat in a clock in a suitcase
passing through airport security.
I risked so much, it's beyond me.

Beer

Like the life of the mind,

        beer pushes suds.

It spins a halo—so happy to see us—

        and begins its frothy ascension

of luxury cream:

        Venus lifting the foam mattress.

And then, a little Niagara,

        beer comes to a decision—

you can't say you weren't warned—

        and you're mopping

the table like you're

        wiping spray from a trough

while panning for gold.

        Or sopping up, with a cocktail napkin,

an evaporating mermaid.

        And then, returning to the glass,

you lift a torch doused in the surf of time.

        This is your brew against subtlety.

This fluff thickens eye lids,

        puts us on a low, low setting,

and hauls the perfumed barge

        of sleep in its wake.

Then, in a flourish,

      beer signs its name

with the legend:

      You there,

you with your throat in a lather,

      I am dread's quencher,

anxiety's antidote,

      guilt's blotter.

You. You've had enough

      existence for one day.

No One Rides the Jelly Fish Home

Saddle bags blown out of hell's vents!
As if the moon blew up with laughter
and plugged rivets in the face of the water...
Also a plastic bag high on a branch
across from the highway
and a fleecy ringworm under a dome.
But who am I to call names?
I too was once a cloud deep in the ocean.
I too was once the poor dumb runaway
mule of the ocean.
I too once turned myself inside out.
But I was never pornography for our time,
or a slow motion rampage.
Never the jelly that quivers the fish.
Or so I said to the agents who read my email
and tapped my phone.
Although soon enough they gave up in disgust
after my fourth metaphor:
Leave her alone! they cried.
She's destroying the language for us!

Gertrude Stein as the White Rabbit
Visits Colette

You're not going to be late, are you?
The garden path is lovely,

if you have enough of a garden
to hold a path.

So why not wear a watch and a waistcoat
and meet those acrobat-trained hands?

I remember the plush, the powder,
a peach dimpled with rainwater,

to deliquesce, to mask, to tighten a chin strap.
The body was not an excuse

and not a set of blocks.
The beret on the head squashed,

a disguise that hid lead around the eyes.
She wore leggings like kindling.

A rabbit's shadow is a walrus.
We're late—just open the hutch.

So many important dates,
who can remember them all?

To reappear as a powder puff
with a heart thumping inside it.

So many ways to live
within a face,

to take your body to lunch,
to carry around a hole in the ground

and disappear in it.

To Be Blameless Is to Be Miniature

I'm making my imaginary dinner
        balanced on a drop of water.
    That button: it's a platter.

That raspberry-sized pillow on
        the playing-card bed.
    Of course no one eats.

No one sleeps.
        No one gets comfortable here.
    You cannot stand inside innocence.

But the mind moves from room to room,
        trains first on these dimensions:
    I slide furniture around.

I lift the shower stall,
        the book so small it can't be read,
    the wheelbarrow for an acorn,

all these little near nothings.
        No doors in this house, this open house,
    the only way in is pity.

The Blouse

The day I wore the blouse
both men who didn't care for me the day before,

both, as if reading from the same script, said:
I didn't recognize you today.

In tones of approval.
I thought: it has something to do with the blouse.

I must have been dressed in luck, a dark blue.
The men, attentive now,

they were the ones who were different.
But I liked the difference too.

Later, a group of us went to a party.
The apartment had a balcony, breezes were soft.

I began to feel sad about the blouse.
What was it about the blouse

that wasn't about me?
It was years before I turned thirty.

Should I simply have been grateful
and forgotten the day before and all

the days before the blouse?
What turns luck, turns words,

never to know entirely what's likely or unlikely,
if it has something to do with the blouse.

Balanced

Once I tried to balance things out.
With the shy I talked too much.

With the arrogant I became humble.
With the humble I acted as if I were humbler,

which is a kind of arrogance.
You didn't thank me

so I thanked you.
You flirted with my husband

so I pretended to like you.
Well? What to say?

Something in me loved shapeliness.
I thought I could make up for

what any occasion lacked.
Such as this:

I am having a wonderful time,
especially if you aren't.

The Coast of Apples

I would fly to the coast of apples.
—Euripides, trans. Frederick Morgan

When I flew to the coast of ghosts,
there, on the white branch, sat Euripides.
At once, I tried to peel the skin

off my own anxiety. Euripides,
I said, you with the glorious name,
what do you want with apples

now? Flying, I can understand.
Although there are problems enough.
I've flown every month

for a year. Too often my flight was detoured
to the coast of bullets, the coast of salt,
the coast of abandoned tires—

which is not much better than flying
to the coast of thistles
but preferable to the coast of briars

next to the coast of radioactive waste.
At last when I stopped talking
Euripides peered down and said to me:

I bet the wings were the hardest part.
That, and the rest of the horse.

Saving St. Sebastian

Only later will there be

a flight in reverse,
arrows plucked and stacked
in a widow's den.

By then he's a man made
of loops, sieves.
A map of quills,

recovering in time
to insult the emperor.
At which point he'll be beaten,

tossed in a pit. He'll
die of that, not arrows.
For now,

taking him down
from the post,
he's tight as a drumskin.

Later, artists will flay a lily,
not him.
And make

an occasion
for a gleaming torso
to purify torture.

The Defeatists

They're looking for
disappointment.
They don't even find it.
They have a talent
they turn away from
as if Lot's wife
obeyed her husband.

They never ask,
Why did the hive
smoke its own honey?
Or: When did the drones
slide over our own cities,
bored by warfare?
At most the defeatists say:

We're not out of the woods yet.
Not out of words.
Our words turn to wood.
Our woods to stores.
Our words are wooden with stores.
You can buy anything here:
we're not even out of wars.

Suit of Armor

This is a skinned man.
The rain rolls off a thistle
in a field of guillotines.
A smoldering pelt of silver.
Like a river in spring
seen under grey clouds,
the metal blood
hammered into lungs.
The dense shine buffed.
They did their work
like children in costumes.
Nothing inside the hollow now,
not even a draft.
The body is a refugee.
A tureen of guts.
Who scrubbed out the boy?

Snow

There are the stories of the weaker body

saved by being swallowed

into a ravine

or turned into a stream or a spattering of stars.

But then punishment meant transformation too.

So hard to know what a gesture means.

*

The ancient, sordid story of Daphne the laurel:

legs joined, fluttering slim

leaf flickerings. And yet in that instant of change

each artery raying out.

To know her body as an extremity:

fingertips budding,

and then to be faceless,

blinded but not before having inhabited

green shuddering arms,

turning this way and that,

and the disappointed face she sees last,

not imagining the human

to dance without moving her feet.

Better to think the story is a mask

and Daphne walked away
in her human body.
And thus the true story has never been told:
the last one you want to tell the truth:
a god who didn't get his way.

*

For years I talked less of snow
than of spring.

Type it and your fingers gallop: snow snow snow snow snow.

You're just sitting there but you're running away.

*

I've lost what I meant
to say to you.
Where is the ghost to light our way
out of the abandoned house,
the small cold rooms?
The wrong address, mail delivered.
I opened the package.

The women made to look

like little girls, pubic hair shaved.

The chill morning light fell through

the magazine.

It is legal

to look like a little girl

and to look at women

who look like little girls.

The truth about the doctor,

I would not have realized the truth, perhaps, until

the caller. How he examined girls.

The caller, outraged in the doctor's defense, wanted

my name on a petition to defend him.

This was many years ago.

I hadn't known that what he did was wrong.

A crime I had no name for at nineteen.

*

I write a story about a woman

who doesn't want to be touched.

It makes no sense

to those who read it.

I take classes at night, work as a typist during the day

in a credit agency.

Eight cups of coffee,

then ten,

and still I fall asleep at my desk.

At night I take

courses in demography,

whatever fits into my schedule.

I write a story about a student

who takes courses in demography. Otherwise,

it's not my life, which is, in this instance,

like hers, about

individuals, not populations.

*

The mothers were asked to make book bags.

Mine was made from an old tablecloth.

Nothing I believed could be as beautiful.

Of that I was convinced,

carrying the bag over my shoulder, yellow book bag,

a wax tablecloth book bag.

I was almost embarrassed by its beauty. It must glow.

Put all others to shame. The golden fleece.

From that one incident so much of my life followed,

a measure of beauty—and yet every other

book bag was more beautiful, I knew.

Still, that book bag.

The other book bags belonged to the other world,

not my world. My world of beauty.

The saved world.

To do things right

as right is agreed upon,

you can have no end point,

no point.

Believe what you want

she was not a laurel.

*

I learned last night that a man died,

someone I feared for years.

He died younger by years

and even now I'm afraid to conjure him.

I am not conjuring him. He is not rooted

anywhere. I used myself to free myself.

Which mostly means: luck.

I remember him shouting into my face.

I remember how falling apart seemed a way to make him leave,

how when I left

I feared he would climb through the window with a knife.

I was a college girl

and went to a counselor.

You must be imagining he would hurt you, she said.

Sometimes I think I've forgotten something,

that somewhere there's another apartment

and now I must pay the rent

and something is forgotten there,

someone or some animal

that would die without my care.

The first time he left handprints like evidence on my back.

Another time he was stopped

because shouts came from a porch

and he pulled back. Another time:

a security guard came

and the boy was astonished I had called for help

as his hands closed on my neck.

You wonder—or, to be more precise, I wonder—

what could have happened

if I hadn't escaped.

I only escaped because

he wasn't interested in me anymore.

*

Where are the snows of yesteryear?

Those needle blasts and white outs

that landed like diligent hens,

the bone hoops,

the silk wetted,

or the winded orchard,

or the pink flakes glittering

around the cement factory,

or the plunging draft horses of snow,

years of snow, snow of years,

no two years alike.

When did we learn to put on our own coat,

our own gloves? Our own legs,

our own arms?

Where is the accounting for our years,

painted here in snow light,

the thicker snow, thickening in

purple drifts, the years of snow,

little Moscow of Michigan.

Salome's Dance

She was a rabbitty teenager punked out in
polka dots, her feet nicking the air.
This baby in her sword dance, this blotted peeler,
this little-bitty trotter with a blind spot.
She pared down into slots.
She judged how far to go to make sure
the bird got shot. She danced

like shower curtains,
like a swizzle stick, savannah wrapped,
twirling her seven pajamas.
That platter needs a head, she said,
take it all off.
Who wouldn't follow the twists of her silly tickler pack?
Her beads clicked like a respirator.

She draped the ribbon-cutting ceremony
for psychopaths.
Her feet were pattering clams and her arms
snakes in a birdcage, wind scalping a rooftop.
Through it all, how innocent her face was.
A face:
that catch basin.

Miss Jessel

—*The Turn of the Screw*

Without human attention a spirit turns crayfish-cold
and like a crayfish bloats on corpses.

We bloat on fear's fantasies.
See the governess sailing across the grounds,

practically overblown in her bone hoops?
She'll pause at the fountain.

Once my life was a fountain
with a shattered mirror in it.

Who could see what was wrong with me?
A fountain is helpless to draw glass shards from itself.

I was with a man made of bedrooms and windows.
But it was a mirror that gave me the most misery.

Mrs. Macbeth

No greater romantic adventure exists than to have loved
Lady Macbeth with true and directly felt love.
—Fernando Pessoa (trans. Richard Zenith)

She curses at her own hands
when it was her tongue in the man.
Do it for your name,

for the owl in the vanity mirror:
soft bodied, blood winded,
flute spotted,

murder's birdy
combing her feathers.
Somebody's been sitting in my chair!

And she's speaking to you:
You, you flabby-
hearted creature

and unheated gestation.
To love the mouth that only
guilt savors: soup in a sponge.

You who would dig
a soapy grave.
You bubble pipe for ambition.

The Shadow Must Find Its Shadow

The shadow wants to climb walls,
to escape above the bed,
to escape being sewn like a veil.
Even a shadow must tear at last,
retract its necklace of skulls and bats.
Until then, the shadow adores the wall
and prefers not to be without it.
It's the shadow of a bear
as much as of a boy,
yet wilder than a bear or a boy.
Even a shadow wants its liberty
free of the body that bore it,
free of its little father.

The Weak Already Inherited

Pussy willows budded warheads this year—
that was the forsythia's job.

Maybe the water buffalo like
being overturned by the scallops—

has anyone ever thought of that?
The prawns set a precedent,

torching twice as many cars as last month.
(Remember the egg that broke into the deli

to revenge its mother?
It never could be restrained.)

Butterflies advanced without mercy.
Newborns: the snipers

most likely to pick us off.
Those toothpicks sure took out

their frustrations on the submarine.
That rainbow made quick work

of muscling in on the lucrative drug trade.
Weird about the oysters renting that outsized chalet

in Switzerland
just to manipulate worldwide oil prices.

And you. I hope you have a license
for those tear drops.

Modesty

is so boring.
Something I think it is
monstrously boring.

Megalomania,
on the other hand,
is even more boring,

although arrogance is tolerable
in some people—
although none

I've met.
Sometimes
haughty disdain

is refreshing.
It says, I don't need you,
and we say—

too much.
For instance,
when your high horse ate hay

all through our lunch,
I paid the bill,
the tip too, and only then

backed out of the tent
where Scheherazade herself,
the patron saint of suspense,

kept on telling her stories
to her murderer-prince.
He salted a lot of virgins

with his contempt.
Poor her. Poor purveyor of delay.
At some level

she could do nothing for him.
Neither could have
Chekhov.

A Winter's Midsummer Night's Dream

As if the summer breezes were ground

slowly and hardened,

ice beads pelt the bower

plunking on the donkey's head.

The cherry blossoms glaze and dip.

Chilled steam slides from those bat-wing sleeves,

and spirits turn away from spells

in favor of clairvoyance without yearning—

they clip off the fake cowslip,

unenchanted by enchantment.

No rhetoric waits in reserve.

They turn out the cobwebs

and sweep from their ring

any bloody thing that was lured.

They give a child away to a herd.

The Clues

The woven reeds, the slats
in the middle of the path—
with the book bag, the shoe,
the empty basket.

Then, the mixed prints in the woods.
Hair shredded on a bush.
Fibers, red and black.
So much for forensics to do,

it wasn't until well past two
when we found our way
to the end of the path.
There in a cottage

rocked the girl and her family,
sipping tea. Just over their heads
a wolf pelt rippled,
the eyes spinning

in the skinned skull
regarding that domestic economy.
Three generations:
the mother, once out of the story,

now back, with her own daughter,
plus her own mother,
plus two baskets of snacks.
And all of them—that girl and those women—

brimming with so much liberty
none of them even bothered
to turn to the wall and gloat
at that patch of furry kitsch:

Just look at us,
you son of a bitch.

Hunger Song

Hunger
      is first
      and hunger is last.
Hunger
      makes a woman
      push children from her house.
Hunger
      sends birds
      to eat the children's path.
Hunger
      draws children
      to nibble at sugar's house.
Hunger
      opens a door
      to let the children in.
Hunger
      makes a caged
      child grow thin.
Hunger
      pushes a woman
      over the oven's rim.
Hunger
      never loses
      her children.

Winter Pool of Carp

At first a scald,
then a cataract skimmed back,

and then a gray rippling Turkish Delight
below which hang

fingerlings of scraped gold bric-a-brac
until our neighbor

hammers the sky
and the carp slide around like old style

souls in old style hell,
under ever-hardening heaven.

Shots of Vodka

Sausage: rumored to mitigate the effects of vodka

First comes sausage, next comes vodka.
Like a layer of packed dirt abused by a coffin,
the sausage waits in the stomach for vodka.

Another shot! A lingering sting
from medicinal history.
Solved: the mystery of your education!

Funny how you never saw vodka
knock you flat.
But then you get up.
You get up and you walk.

You walk until you meet a pig.
And you know what you're like when you meet a pig.
You apologize to the pig for his future

drilled by vodka. The pig speaks softly.
He says he's heard he's not headed for sausage.
Instead, he will be roasted

with an apple in his mouth.
Why, he asks? Why do they put
an apple in my mouth

as if after I'm dead I'm still eating?
If it's realism they want
they should feed me garbage.

There is nothing you can say to the talking pig.
It's not realism you want.

Beauty

A mother kept her daughter hidden from the Russian. A stranger,
the Russian raised his gun above the table and shot through the oil
painting of a card shark. *That man cheats!* the Russian shouted. It's still there:
the bullet hole. Was the stranger proving he was honest when it came to
cards? Nevertheless, the mother knew enough to hide beauty.

Wait. Then wait more.
Until danger's out of the house.
Hide beauty.
Then, dear God, double beauty.
Invent sisters.

Gather Ye Rosebuds While Ye May

Like there's another choice for ye.
Gather ye rosebuds when you can't.
Impossible happiness, gather.
In this town if you want
breathable air
you stand in the square
with a sign around your neck.
The sign says Whiner.
The roses gather in mobs. The mobs
are in favor of mob rule.
Look at those rosebuds, gathering.
Ye rosebuds, flakey
beauties sobbing, fitful, gather.
Bedraggled in a gutter, hosed.
Snap, deliver.
Gather, ye, may ye
while ye bud
before you are gathered in rosebuds.

Notes

"During the Victorian Era Women Often Fell into Holes" is for CeCe Ziolkowski.

"A Terrarium" is dedicated in memory of Lana Upton Kaltz.

In a 1963 letter Flannery O'Connor described the interior of a bottled cross given to her by Elizabeth Bishop: "It is an altar with Bible, chalice and two fat candles on it, a cross above this with a ladder and the instruments of the crucifixtion [sic] hung on it, and on top of the cross a rooster. It's all wood except the altar cloth and the rooster and these are paper, painstakingly cut out and a trifle dirty from the hands that did it. Anyway, it's very much to my taste..." (*Letters of Flannery O'Connor: The Habit of Being* 519). O'Connor and Bishop spoke once by phone, corresponded, but never met.

"Far Country" is for Theodora Bishop.

"Beauty" is for Yetta Ziolkowski.

About the Author

Lee Upton is the author of five previous books of poetry including *Undid in the Land of Undone*, *Civilian Histories*, and *Approximate Darling*; the story collection *The Tao of Humiliation*; the essay collection *Swallowing the Sea: On Writing & Ambition, Boredom, Purity & Secrecy*; the novella *The Guide to the Flying Island*; and several books of critical prose, most recently *Defensive Measures: The Poetry of Niedecker, Bishop, Glück, and Carson*. She is a professor of English and the writer-in-residence at Lafayette College.